ALASKA

A Photo Memory

Published by Todd Communications
203 W. 15th Ave., Suite 102
Anchorage, Alaska 99501-5128
Phone: (907) 274-8633
Fax: (907) 276-6858
e-mail: info@toddcom.com

Copyright 1999 Todd Communications,
Anchorage, Alaska

Editor: Flip Todd
Designers: Wendy Stevens & Tina Wallace
Text & Captions: Janice Berry

Photography: Randy Brandon
                Laurent Dick
                Mark Kelley

Printed in Korea by Samhwa Printing Co., Ltd.

20 19 18 17 16 15 14 13 12 11 10 9 8 7

The motor vessel *LeConte* sails through Olga Strait after departing Sitka. Alaska Marine Highway ferries travel from Bellingham, Washington to Prince Rupert, British Columbia, Canada as well as Ketchikan, Petersburg, Wrangell, Juneau, Haines and Skagway in Alaska's "banana belt" Panhandle. Other state ferries also go to smaller towns in Southeast Alaska, as well as Valdez, Cordova, Whittier, Seward, Homer and Kodiak.

ALASKA

A Photo Memory

3

As snow inches down the Chugach Mountains toward Anchorage, winter is not far away.

Anchorage

Anchorage began as a tent city in 1915, when the site was selected as the headquarters of the Alaska Railroad. It is now the largest city in Alaska with a population of more than 260,000.

Hot air balloons drift over Anchorage's annual Fur Rendezvous Festival in February that brightens the cold, dark winter days.

Next Page
Anchorage is bordered by the Chugach Mountains to the east, the Cook Inlet to the west and Elmendorf Air Force Base to the north.

Photo © **Randy Brandon**

Photo © **Randy Brandon**

The setting sun casts its fading rays on the 22-story Arco and Bank of America buildings in front of the Chugach Mountains.

Photo © **Randy Brandon**

The 127-mile Seward Highway connects Anchorage with Seward on the Kenai Peninsula.

Photo © Randy Brandon

Photo © Randy Brandon

Fishing boats fill the harbor at Kodiak, a major fisheries port on the second largest island under the American flag.

Seward

Bainbridge Passage is host to a colorful spring sunset in Prince William Sound.

Photo © Randy Brandon

The small boat harbor in Seldovia is home to a commercial fishing fleet.

Photo © Randy Brandon

Dwarf fireweed *(Epilobium latifolium)* grow in an outcrop next to Exit Glacier near Seward.

Photo © **Randy Brandon**

Motorists enjoy panoramic views along the Parks Highway in the Tanana River Valley south of Fairbanks.

At the foot of 3,022-foot Mount Marathon is Seward, the southern terminus of the Alaska Railroad.

Photo © **Laurent Dick**

9

Photo © **Randy Brandon**

Caribou *(Rangifer tarandus)* forage on the tundra as a wind surfer skims across a lake near Prudhoe Bay.

Wildlife

A willow ptarmigan *(Lagopus lagopus)* is well camouflaged against the snow in its winter plumage.

A large humpback whale *(Megaptera novaeangliae)* dives into the waters of the Kenai Fjords National Park.

Sea otters *(Enhydra lutris)* propel themselves through the water with webbed hind feet and have water repellent fur, the densest of any mammal.

A cow moose *(Alces alces)* feeds on vegetation in a pond in Denali National Park and Preserve.

Photo © Randy Brandon

The Chiswell Islands are a popular breeding site for Steller sea lions *(Eumetopias jubatus)*.

Photo © Randy Brandon

Dall sheep *(Ovis dalli)* are the world's only white wild sheep and can only be found in Alaska and Canada.

11

Photo © Randy Brandon

Boats, Glaciers & More

Valdez's small boat harbor sits on the north side of 12-mile-long Valdez Arm, a deep, saltwater fjord in northeast Prince William Sound.

Photo © **Randy Brandon**

Commercial fishing boats are rafted together in the small boat harbor on the Homer Spit in Kachemak Bay.

Photo © **Randy Brandon**

St. Nicholas Russian Orthodox Chapel in Kenai was built in 1906.

Photo © Randy Brandon

Russian Orthodox Transfiguration of Our Lord Church is located in Ninilchik on the Kenai Peninsula.

Photo © Randy Brandon

Cottonwood *(Populus balsamifera)* leaves reflect fall's fading daylight below Explorer Glacier in Portage Valley, 50 miles from Anchorage.

Photo © Randy Brandon

Pioneer Peak overlooks a farm in the fertile Matanuska Valley 40 miles north of Anchorage.

Previous Page
Holgate Glacier calves into the
sea in Kenai Fjords National Park.

Photo © Randy Brandon

Tundra swans *(Cygnus columbianus)* swim at Potter Marsh south of Anchorage near Turnagain Arm.

Photo © **Randy Brandon**

Aspen *(Populus tremuloides)*, the most widely distributed tree species in North America, wear fall foliage near the Sterling Highway on the Kenai Peninsula.

Photo © **Randy Brandon**

Photo © Randy Brandon

A rapidly retreating Columbia Glacier, more than 40 miles long, terminates at the head of Columbia Bay on Prince William Sound.

Next Page
Late summer has come to
Mt. McKinley in the Alaska
Range overlooking Wonder
Lake in Denali National
Park and Preserve.

Photo © Randy Brandon

Two-mile long Lost Lake sits at an elevation of 2,000 feet on the Kenai Peninsula near Seward.

Photo © Randy Brandon

Tour buses stop at Stony Hill pullout, 61 miles into the Denali National Park and Preserve, to give passengers a good view of Mt. McKinley.

Mt. McKinley, or Denali, dwarfs all wildlife, including a large bull caribou (*Rangifer tarandus*).

Denali

Sporting a full rack, a bull moose (*Alces alces*) feeds in a pond near Wonder Lake.

Photo © Randy Brandon

Oblivious to a tour bus full of curious visitors, a caribou *(Rangifer tarandus)* trots across the road in Denali National Park and Preserve.

Next Page
The Matanuska Glacier spills out of the Chugach Mountains as fall foliage frames the icy mass.

Photo © Randy Brandon

Photo © Laurent Dick

Chum (dog) salmon hang on racks to dry at a fish camp along the Yukon River near the Athabaskan Indian village of Tanana.

A cow moose *(Alces alces)* feeds on plants from Wonder Lake at dusk with Mt. McKinley on the horizon.

Photo © Randy Brandon

Photo © Laurent Dick

Photo © Laurent Dick

Clockwise from top left
Reflection Pond mirrors a towering Mt. McKinley on the horizon at Denali National Park and Preserve.

A climber pauses high on Mt. McKinley's West Buttress with 17,400-foot Mt. Foraker in the distance in Denali National Park and Preserve.

Climbers ascend the summit ridge leading to the 20,320-foot South Peak of Mt. McKinley.

Photo © Laurent Dick

Photo © Laurent Dick

Photo © Laurent Dick

Clockwise from top left
The midnight sun illuminates the north face of 14,573-foot Mt. Hunter on a summer's night.

The moon rises above Mt. Hunter in the Alaska Range.

Mountain climbers celebrate victory with a "summit song" on the top of Mt. McKinley.

Photo © Laurent Dick

 A grizzly bear in Denali National Park and Preserve uses a highway safety cone for a toy.

A mature bull caribou *(Rangifer tarandus)* stands on the tundra at the Gates of the Arctic National Park and Preserve in Alaska's Brooks Range.

Denali Wildlife

A grizzly bear *(Ursus arctos)* wanders a lonely stretch of highway in Alaska's Interior.

The McNeil River provides for both food (silver salmon) and drink for a young brown bear *(Ursus arctos)*.

A male caribou *(Rangifer tarandus)* browses on the fall tundra near Wonder Lake.

Photo © Randy Brandon

Photo © Randy Brandon

A lean female wolf *(Canis lupus)* uses her superior senses of sight and smell to hunt for caribou.

Photo © Randy Brandon

Part of the Western Arctic Caribou Herd, which at 500,000 is the largest in Alaska, crosses the Brooks Range during its annual fall migration.

Photo © Laurent Dick

Wildlife

A Dall sheep *(Ovis dalli)* ram grazes on a ridge in Denali National Park and Preserve.

Photo © Laurent Dick

Transportation

An Alaska Railroad train crosses through the Alaska Range near Denali State Park.

Photo © Randy Brandon

A rusted locomotive rests on tracks of the long-defunct 15-mile Yakutat and Southern Line that carried salmon from the Situk River to a cannery and deepwater port at Yakutat.

Photo © Laurent Dick

Photo © Laurent Dick

Photo © Laurent Dick

Photo © Laurent Dick

Photo © Laurent Dick

Clockwise from top left
A floatplane provides easy access to Iniakuk Lake located in the Gates of the Arctic National Park.

The sternwheeler Discovery III paddles on the Chena River, continuing four generations of river navigation by the Binkley family of Fairbanks.

A fishwheel along the Yukon River near Tanana provides salmon for both dogs and people.

Frank Turner of Whitehorse, Yukon, Canada drives an eager team at the start of the annual 1,000-mile Yukon Quest International Sled Dog Race in Fairbanks.

Nex Page
The trans-Alaska pipeline carries crude oil through the Alaska Range near Isabel Pass. Raised sections of pipe are usually above permafrost.

Photo © Laurent Dick

An Alaska Railroad locomotive pulls its load through Broad Pass.

Photo © Laurent Dick

Photo © Laurent Dick

Photo © Laurent Dick

The Chatanika Gold Dredge has stood silent for decades as a reminder of the large-scale Tanana basin gold mining that took place in the 1940s. The dredge is located 20 miles northeast of Fairbanks.

The trans-Alaska pipeline runs like a snake toward the Alaska Range near the Richardson Highway south of Delta Junction.

Solid Ground

Photo © Randy Brandon

A Dall sheep *(Ovis dalli)* rests in a sheltered area high above a tundra plateau in Denali National Park and Preserve.

Food is safe from hungry bears in a trapper's cache near Broad Pass.

Photo © Randy Brandon

Caribou antlers and dog sleds litter the yard of a moss-covered cabin at Kantishna.

34

Photo © Laurent Dick

An abandoned cabin sits on the banks of the Yukon River near the Canadian border.

Photo © Laurent Dick

Photo © Laurent Dick

The historic Kennecott Copper Mine is located in the Wrangell-St. Elias National Park and Preserve. The mine operated for 25 years until 1938.

A hiker takes in the view overlooking Gorge Creek in the Denali National Park and Preserve.

35

Photo © Laurent Dick

Cars drive along Cushman Street in downtown Fairbanks during the fleeting daylight hours of winter.

Photo © Laurent Dick

The University of Alaska is headquartered in Fairbanks with a 2,500-acre campus and 8,000 students.

Photo © Laurent Dick

Fairbanks

Aspen trees *(Populus tremuloides)* add brilliant fall color to the Tanana River Basin near Fairbanks.

Photo © Laurent Dick

Fairbanks sprawls beneath the Alaska Range at sunrise. Alaska's second largest community has a population of about 85,000.

Photo © Laurent Dick

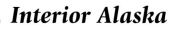

Stairway Icefall cascades down a slope near the head of Root Glacier in Wrangell-St. Elias National Park and Preserve.

Photo © Laurent Dick

Alpenglow from the Endicott Mountains is reflected in the calm waters of the Gates of the Arctic National Park and Preserve.

The lowbush cranberry (*Vaccinium vitis-idaea*) grows in dry alpine tundra along the Dalton Highway north of Fairbanks near Finger Mountain.

Photo © Laurent Dick

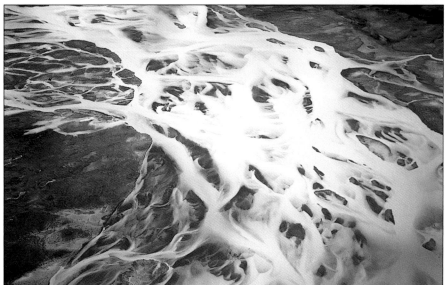

Photo © Laurent Dick

Glacier-fed Skolai Creek winds a path through Wrangell-St.Elias National Park and Preserve.

Photo © Laurent Dick

Mt. Redoubt is an active volcano on the west side of the Cook Inlet that stands 10,197 feet in the Lake Clark National Park and Preserve.

Mountain peaks tower above a glacial valley in Wrangell-St. Elias National Park and Preserve, the largest national park in the United States.

Photo © Laurent Dick

A Yupik Eskimo dance group performs at the annual Festival of Native Arts in Fairbanks. Yupik Eskimos live in coastal Alaska mostly from Unalakleet south to Bristol Bay.

Inupiaq Eskimos from Barrow perform to the beat of drums at the Festival of Native Arts in Fairbanks.

Photo © Laurent Dick

Caribou antlers lie on the tundra
near the headwaters of the Alatna
River in Gates of the Arctic
National Park and Preserve.

Pacific loons *(Gavia pacifica)* are a
common sight on Interior and
northern Alaska lakes where they
migrate to breed and nest each spring.

Next Page
The Mendenhall Glacier is less than 15 miles from Juneau. Moose Lake reflects the fall colors of the surrounding mountainside.

Photo © **Mark Kelley**

Two young brown bears *(Ursus arctos)* catch chum (dog) salmon at McNeil River State Game Sanctuary.

Photo © **Randy Brandon**

A cross-phase red fox *(Vulpes vulpes)* pauses in a snowfield in Alaska's Interior.

Photo © **Randy Brandon**

Photo © Mark Kelley

Photo © Mark Kelley

Ice & Snow

Clockwise from top left
Rafters on the Mendenhall River
get a good view of the
Mendenhall Glacier, descending
from the immense Juneau
Icefield on the Canadian border.

Herbert Glacier near Juneau juts
skyward with jagged spines below
a touring helicopter.

A hiker explores an ice cave inside
Nuggett Glacier near Juneau.

Photo © Mark Kelley

Next Page
A pair of cruise vessels lay at rest in the Gastineau Channel in front of Juneau, Alaska's state capital, only accessible by ship or air.

Photo © **Mark Kelley**

The Ptarmigan chair lift takes skiers to the top of Juneau's Eaglecrest Ski Area on Douglas Island.

Photo © **Mark Kelley**

Photo © **Mark Kelley**

Cathedral Peak rises above Haines. Nearby thousands of bald eagles *(Haliaeetus leucocephalus)* gather to feed on Chilkat River salmon each winter where springs keep the rapidly moving river from freezing solid.

45

The governor's mansion in Juneau has housed Alaska's chief executives since 1913.

Cities & Towns

Sitka is rich in Russian influences including St. Michael's Russian Orthodox Cathedral, first constructed in 1816.

Photo © Mark Kelley

The Mt. Roberts Tram gives rides above Juneau for first-class views of the Gastineau Channel and the historic gold mining town.

Photo © Mark Kelley

Photo © Mark Kelley

Photo © Mark Kelley

Mt. Edgecumbe, an active volcano 9,000 years ago, is only 16 miles west of Sitka.

Photo © Mark Kelley

The former Russian capital of Alaska, Sitka, and its airport lie below Harbor Mountain and advancing storm clouds.

The setting sun silhouettes 3,201-foot Mt. Edgecumbe, a dormant volcano near Sitka.

Photo © Mark Kelley

49

An Alaska Marine Highway System ferry cruises toward a rainbow among islands in Southeast Alaska.

The Port of Cordova located on Prince William Sound is not connected by road to the rest of the state and is largely dependent on salmon fishing to sustain its economy. Until 1938 it was an export point for the Kennecott Copper Mine's Copper River and Northwestern Railroad

Kayakers paddle along Ketchikan Creek near Creek Street in Ketchikan, where many buildings are perched on stilts.

Three boys enjoy a carefree day at Hammer Slough in Petersburg, a fishing community with Norwegian roots.

Next Page
Humpback whales (*Megaptera novaeangliae*) are the most acrobatic species of these mammoth mammals.
A humpback whale in Icy Strait displays its fluke slapping before a dive.

Horse-drawn buggies still carry passengers on the downtown streets of Skagway, a town that came to life during the Klondike Gold Rush.

Proud children hold up a 35-pound king salmon.

Photo © Mark Kelley

Way of Life

A brown bear *(Ursus arctos)* wades through Pack Creek on Admiralty Island.

Photo © Mark Kelley

Three very dark Admiralty Island brown bears enjoy a grassy meal. Alaska's second largest island has only brown bears and is called "Kootznoowoo" by the Tlingit Indians, which means "fortress of the bears."

Photo © Mark Kelley

Fishermen angle for salmon on the shore of False Outer Point with the Chilkat Mountains in the background.

Photo © Mark Kelley

Mature bald eagles *(Haliaeetus leucocephalus)* perch in a tree in the Alaskan Chilkat Bald Eagle Preserve near the Indian village of Klukwan. The bald eagle received its name from American colonists when "bald" or "balled" meant white, not hairless.

Photo © Mark Kelley

Japanese tourist Tetsuya Sato shows a Dungeness crab *(Cancer magister)* he caught near Admiralty Island.

Photo © Mark Kelley

Two harbor seals *(Phoca vitulina)* rest on an iceberg in Tracy Arm-Fords Terror National Wilderness, 40 miles south of Juneau.

Photo © Mark Kelley

A pair of humpback whales breach in Icy Strait in front of a respectful kayaker.

Photo © Mark Kelley

Humpback whales *(Megaptera novaeangliae)* lunge feed by the *Sea Lion* cruise ship in Icy Strait.

Photo © Mark Kelley

Charlie Jimmie from Haines, a Tlingit Indian, dances with the Geesan Dancers at Celebration 90 in Juneau.

Photo © Mark Kelley

Totem poles decorate the path to the Chief Shakes Island tribal house in Wrangell.

Photo © Mark Kelley

Next Page
The Alaska state ferry *Matanuska* rides high at the Skagway dock. Alaska's Marine Highway System names its vessels for glaciers and connects the major communities of Southeast Alaska.

Photo © Mark Kelley

Mountain ash, hawthorne and lilacs frame a totem pole next to the Juneau-Douglas City Museum.

Photo © Mark Kelley

A salmon troller works the waters of Soapstone Point in Cross Sound beneath a rainbow.

Photo © Mark Kelley

A day boat cruises in front of Lamplugh Glacier in Glacier Bay National Park.

Photo © Mark Kelley

60

The Holland America cruise ship *Noordam* pauses in front of the active Margerie Glacier in the Glacier Bay National Park.

Next Page
A White Pass & Yukon Route train returns to Skagway from Canada over an old wooden trestle near Tunnel Mountain. The narrow gauge railroad began carrying freight and passengers to Yukon's Whitehorse in 1900 during the Gold Rush.

The *Sitku* passes the jagged ice of South Sawyer Glacier in the Tracy Arm-Fords Terror National Wilderness.